The Life of an Inmate:

Crime: Capital Murder (True Story)

By: Cicely "Cece" Vance
Cailyn Marie Marshall
Romarcus Deon Marshall

DEDICATION

I would like to dedicated this book to all the inspiring publicists
out there trying to make a way or find themselves into the
wonderful world of
Public Relations
I welcome you with open arms and full armor.......

ACKNOWLEDGMENTS

The death penalty issue is obviously a divisive one. But whether one is for or against, you can not deny the basic illogical – if we know the system is flawed, if we know there are innocent people on Death Row, then until the system is reformed, should we not abandon the death penalty to protect those who are innocent?

CONTENTS

<u>Investigative Activity</u> :

1 THE CALL FROM HIS MOTHER

I remember the day when I got the phone called from Christopher's mother January 5, 2000. Let me take you back November 1999 I was leaving for Detroit my youngest son was born prematurely which I had him on October 29,1999. I packed up everything the same day my son was release from the hospital we was well on our way to start a new life in a different state. At the time my kids was 4, 2, 1 and a newborn. It took us 3 long days to travel to Detroit my mother move there with her husband and I just wanted to be near my mom being the only child. We arrival to Detroit safe and sound. My kids and I where adjusting to a different state and my mom's new husband. Jamie was a pretty nice man but had hidden agenda. December came and went and I was getting homesick but in my mind I knew this was the right place to be and kepted me focus on raising my kids the right way.. I heard the phone ring my mom picked it up and called me to the phone it was Christopher's mother she asked me if I was sitting down I said sitting down for what I heard in her voice that something was wrong something was terribly wrong as she scream she told me that Christopher was set up and facing life without parole I ask what did he do she said capital murder. I quickly look at my kids and ask myself how I'm I going to tell my kids that there daddy is in jail for life all of the questions ponder

in my head is this truth did he really kill someone. Was I sleeping
with the enemy did I have kids with a murdered. I sat my kids
down and just told them look your daddy is in jail I remember my
oldest son asking mommy what's jail I explain to him its like a
camp but you don't ever get to come home. He said mommy I
won't see my daddy anymore I said no son but we can visit his
camp. Keep in mind I haven't spoken to Christopher in years
when I left Houston I left him.. See Christopher was a bad boy you
know selling drugs and other stuff we just could not see eye to eye
I was what you called a girl good bad boys never want a good
girl.. January 1, 2015 I started to do research on Christopher's
case myself to only find loop holes in the system and I ask myself
could this man be innocent after spending 16 years in prison for
a crime he did not commit...

What you are about to read is true facts from court documents,
witnesses, police offices, the victim wife.. Names have been
change to protect the innocent and the guilty

2 Introduction.

Client request that Investigator assist in the defense of Christopher Smith, Charge in Cause #833990, in the 178th District Court, with capital murder. Client advise that Smith gave a statement to Harris County Sheriff's detectives, implicating himself in the robbery/homicide. Smith said that his statement to the police is incorrect and he took no part in the robbery. Smith claims that the co=defendant, Brad Johnson and Keith Harris came by his house early in the evening and took guns from him. There was a female with the co-defendants names Sam (LNU). Smith said that when he realized that they had taken his guns, he made Sam take when he realized that they had taken his guns, he made Sam take him to where the co-defendants were and stumbled onto the robbery. Smith was not identified by any of the victims. The only evidence against Smith is co-defendant Johnson's confession implicating Smith. Smith own statement, which he claimed he signed without reading. Client requested that investigator interview the defendant, Christopher Smith, in jail in order to obtain more information on the female named Sam so she can be located and interviewed to confirm that the co-defendants stole weapons from Smith's residence. Client advised that Kimberly Smith, the defendant's mother, informed him that there was a woman hanging around with Smith before his arrest by the name of Cynthia (LNU). It is believed that Cynthia may currently be in jail for possessing counterfeit money. Client also requested that Investigator contact and interview Kimberly Smith to see if there is anything she knows about the case that has not been covered.

3 KIMBERLY SMITH INTERVIEW (DEFENDANT'S MOTHER)

Kimberly Smith Interview (Defendant's Mother)
- Christopher told his mother that he was not involved in the incident.
- Smith has no idea who implicated Christopher in the incident.
- Smith once warned Christopher about Keith. Smith did not think he "looked right"
- Christopher former girlfriend is named Cynthia, who is a liar
- Cynthia told Smith two different versions of the incident with which Christopher is charged.
- Smith thought Cynthia was trying to "cover up" something
- Cynthia once tried to have Christopher Killed.
- Smith Feels that Christopher was set up
- The perpetrators who tried to kill Christopher were never apprehended.
- Smith has no idea how to contact Cynthia
- Christopher did mention to her mother Smith that there was a black male with the co-defendants and also a woman who accompanied them to his residence.

Kimberly Smith was interviewed on Monday, August 28, 2000 by

Westly Gammmer.

Smith stated that she does not know much regarding the charges on her son. Christopher keep saying, "They are all trying to say that I killed someone." Smith said that Christopher say, "He did not do it."

Smith stated all that the authorities know about the matter is that Christopher had a gun that was used in the incident and someone (one of the suspect) said, " Chris was involved." Smith has no idea who implicated her son. Smith said that was all Kyle Jones had informed her about the incident.

Smith stated that the way she feels about the entire incident is that anybody else could have been involved rather than Christopher.

Smith stated that she knows Keith. Keith once came to her home, along with Christopher. Smith does not know Brad Johnson.

Smith stated that Keith "did not look right to her". Smith later told Christopher about her feeling toward Keith. Smith said there was something about Keith that she did not like.

Smith stated that Christopher in turn said that Keith was in the band. Smith said that Christopher told her "Mama, you don't need to be carrying on about him (Keith)." Smith said that she thinks the name of the band is "Big Boy's League." This is a band that Christopher started up.

Smith stated that she believes that Brad Johnson was also a member of the band. There are other members of the band, but Smith does not know their names. The band has played in Galveston and other locations around Houston, Texas. Smith stated that she knows Cynthia by first name only. Cynthia is the name of Christopher's former girlfriend. After Christopher had been arrested, Cynthia called Smith and in describing events of that evening said that Christopher had been at the house and Johnson and the others had come over. Christopher had gone into the restroom and Johnson and Keith had gotten some guns etc. Smith stated that Cynthia actually had two different versions of the story. Smith said that she could not believe anything that Cynthia would say.

The second version was that when Johnson and Keith came to the residence of Christopher, Christopher got up, took a shower, put on his clothes and went with them (to do the robbery). Smith stated that she then asked Cynthia "Are you covering up something?" Smith said that Cynthia responded, "No ma'am. No ma'am. Smith stated that approximately one week before the incident she had warned Christopher about her feeling that "someone was out to get him" Smith said that she felt Christopher was "set up" in the incident. Smith would tell this to the police or anyone about her feeling that Christopher was set up.

Smith stated that she felt this way because she be
believed "anyone could be called Chris, Kris, or anything of the

sort." Smith said that instead the police came looking for Christopher. Smith said that she as to wonder to herself "what is up?"

Smith stated that she could tell Christopher really did not like Cynthia very much. Smith described Cynthia as "wild". There were many things that Cynthia did that Smith did not like. Cynthia once tried to have Christopher killed and then bragged about it. Smith said that she does not know who hired whom to do the killing. Christopher was supposed to have been at home. Approximately 15 minutes after Cynthia left the house, two men with hoods came in and tried to kill Christopher. Smith said that afterward she told Christopher, "God was on your side." The perpetrators were never apprehended and nothing else was ever said about the incident. Smith said that Christopher could not give a god description of the perpetrators because they wore long sleeved clothing and had mask. Smith did not know if the men were black or white. Smith said that they shot the ring finger from the right hand of Christopher and also shot him in the shoulder.

Christopher was later taken to Ben Taub Hospital and then to Hermann Hospital. Smith stated that she has no idea why Cynthia would have wanted to have Christopher Killed. Smith has no idea how to get in contact with Cynthia. Smith said that she has tried to contact Cynthia regarding her help in Christopher case and to find out what happened and "who said what." Smith said, "Apparently Cynthia has her own life to live" Smith said that she tried to page Cynthia, but her pager number has changed. Smith stated that all Cynthia did was lie. Smith said that she "just does not like the girl." Smith said that Cynthia forgets what she says. When she does lie, she forgets the lies that she tells.

Smith does not know Cynthia's last name. Smith thought the last name may be Roberts or Wright. Smith is not sure on either point. Smith said that she will see if Christopher can tell her the last name of Cynthia. Smith thought Cynthia had later moved to Tyler, Texas. Christopher once got a letter from Cynthia while in jail, but sent it back because he did not want to read it. Smith said that she believes that Cynthia change her name, but does not know for sure what it is.

End of Interview...

Smith does not think clearly and does not complete her thoughts or her sentence. Smith's thought patterns race from one aspect of the incident (of which she has limited knowledge) to another. Smith does not speak clearly nor in a consistently coherent fashion.

Smith is probably somewhat deceptive and gave the impression that she could not or would not bring herself to believe Christopher may have been involved in the incident.

Smith would make a dubious witness.

4 Christopher Smith Interview

On Tuesday, September 05, 2000, J.J. Grand visited the Harris County jail and interviewed defendant Christopher Smith in person.

Smith stated that Cynthia had been his girlfriend for four years. Initially, Smith could not remember Cynthia's last name. Smith said Cynthia was living with him at the time of the incident. Investigator had to prompt Smith to get him to supply more information about Cynthia. Smith said that Cynthia was 25 years old, short in stature, with a medium build. Smith stated that Cynthia had gone to San Jacinto College, attending the Nursing Program. Smith stated that Cynthia last name was Swanon. Smith did not know how to spell the last name. Smith stated that Cynthia had never been in trouble for counterfeit money. But believed she may have been in jail for bad checks prior to the shooting.

Smith stated that on the night of the shooting, he received a telephone call from Brad Johnson . Johnson told Smith that he was having some problems and wanted to come over and talk with him. Smith said that Cynthia heard him speaking on the phone with Johnson. Smith said that Cynthia was aware that Johnson was coming over to Smith's residence to speak with him.

Smith stated that Cynthia only heard his portion of the conversation. Smith said that nothing was said in Cynthia's presence that would give any indication that he was planning to rob anyone. Smith stated that Cynthia was asleep when Johnson and Harris came over to his apartment. Smith said that Cynthia slept throughout the whole gun-stealing incident. Smith stated that he had known Johnson for a few years, He and Johnson had "done some rapping together." Smith said that he had only seen Harris a few times out in clubs.

Smith stated that he was speaking in the living room with Harris and Johnson when his alarm went off at about 5:00 a.m. Smith said that he went to the bedroom to see if the alarm clock had awoken his daughter. When Smith returned, Johnson and Harris were gone. Smith noticed that the closet door where he kept his . 223 rifle was missing. Smith said that he used to keep the rifle in the closet near the hot water heater. Smith stated that Johnson knew the rifle was in the closet because Johnson had been with Smith when Smith returned home on previous occasions. Smith had a gun carry permit. Smith would take his revolver and put it in the closet next to the rifle. Smith said that Johnson had seem him place the revolver inside the closet on enough occasion to know that the rifle was also stored there. Smith stated that the female named Sam, who had come with Johnson and Harris, was still in her apartment. Smith said that he questioned Sam about what was going on. Sam initially responded that she did not know. Smith said that he kept questioning Sam until she made the statement that she remained behind because "she did not want to be apart of it." Smith said that Sam finally admitted that she "probably knew where Jonson and Harris had gone." Smith stated that he made Sam drive his truck . Sam took him to a location where they found Johnson vehicle. Smith said that he then took out his handgun and exited his vehicle. Smith said that he heard someone yelling. "Police." Smith said that he thought the police were at the location, so he ran and put his gun in the truck. Smith said that he did not want to be in a confrontation with police officers while he was carrying his handgun.

Smith stated that he saw Harris and Johnson by the door of the residence. Smith said that he hard a gunshot. Smith said that he saw Johnson run from the doorway with Smith's rifle in his hand . Smith said that he confronted Johnson and snatched his rifle in his hand. Smith said that he got back in his truck, making Sam drive him back to his residence. Smith said at that point he put up the rifle and his handgun. Smith stated that he then took Sam to Ripplewood because that is where she told him that he could find Johnson and Harris. At this point in the interview, Smith became very vague. Smith said that Ripplewood was a street he dove on, turning off on an unknown street, to an individual's house named Trevor's house. Smith did not know Trevor's last name.

Smith stated that when he arrived at Trevor's house, Sam was still with him. Smith said that he got into an argument with Johnson , who jumped the balcony. Smith said Harris then came outside with a shotgun. Smith said that Harris was pretty skinny. Smith said he grabbed the shotgun from Harris grasp. Smith stated that he then left, leaving Sam behind. Smith stated that Trevor witnessed his altercation with Johnson and Harris. Smith said that Trevor could verify that he was upset that the pair had stolen his rifle . Smith said that Sam was a black female, light skinned, 20 to

30 years of age. Smith could not provide a good description for Trevor.

Investigator tried to obtain additional information regarding Sam identity. Smith said that he had seen Sam on numerous at the various clubs he had visited. Smith said that Sam was always "with lots of dudes." Smith was asked if Johnson was Sam boyfriend. Smith said Sam and Johnson "they be talking." Smith claimed that he had no involvement in the robbery and the attempted robbery/murder. Smith said that he was willing to take a polygraph examination to prove his innocence.

Smith stated that the evening he was apprehended by the Sheriff's Department detectives, he was in his vehicle in his apartment complex parking lot. Smith said that a heavy set black male approached him in plain clothes with a gun in his hand. Smith thought he was about to be robbed. Smith said that as he drove away, the black male fired two rounds into his truck. Smith said that he drove around to the other side of the apartment complex where he saw two Impalas. Smith said at this time he believed the individuals might be police officers, so he stopped and gave himself up. Smith said that police officers told him that his gun had been used in a killing. Smith signed a form to allow the police officers to go up to his apartment and retrieve his rifle. Marshall stated that if he had been involved in the killing, he certainly would have never allowed the police to search his apartment.

At this point in the interview, Investigator tried to direct Smith's attention to his signed statement. Smith stated that he never signed the statement. Smith said that his signature was a forgery. Smith did not know who signed his name to the statement. Smith admitted that the initials on the statement at the beginning and end of each paragraph and at the Miranda Warnings were his.

Investigator asked Smith the identity of the person identified in his statement as Samantha. Smith initially stated that Samantha was Harris. Then Smith changed his story and said that Samantha was actually the female named Chris. Smith was asked who the other black male was that was mentioned in the statement. Smith said that the black male, whose identity he does not know, When Smith was asked why he did not bring this up earlier, Smith stated he did not know the black male had been to his house. Smith stated that when he arrived at the shooting scene, he saw the black male seated in Johnson vehicle. Smith said that he assumed the black male had been at his residence but had remained outside in the vehicle. Smith was asked to explain why he initialed the statement if it was not true. Smith stated that the police officers beat him, so he initialed the statement because he was scared. Smith was asked to explain how the police officers beat him. Smith stated that one of the police officers was very angry that he had run in the apartment complex parking lot. Smith said that one of the police officers struck him in the back of the head with an unknown object as they entered the jail. Smith said that was the only time the police officers stuck him. Smith said that he still had the mark in his head from where he was hit. Smith agreed that the majority of the information in the statement was accurate. But the police had "twisted what he said and created their own version to implicate him." Smith stated that the police officers threatened to file aggravated assault charges on him if he did not initial the statement.

Smith was asked if Cynthia was awake when he returned to the apartment with Sam after the shooting. Smith stated that Cynthia never woke up and had no idea of what was going on. Investigator explained to Smith that it was imperative that Investigator identify and locate the female named Sam. Smith asked why Sam was so important. Investigator explained to Smith that she is the only individual that could support his story about the guns being stolen from his residence. Sam could also explain his presence at the shooting scene.

Smith did not seem too interested in finding Sam, but suggested for the third time that Investigator find and interview Trevor as the one who could support his story.

End of Interview...

Smith did not seem credible at all. It is Investigator's belief that Smith possesses a great of information than he was willing to share. It is hard to believe that Smith does not know much about his girlfriend, Cynthia who lived with him for four years.

- Zepeda was asleep in the back bedroom when the robbery began.
- Someone kicked in the door and ordered him to face down on the floor.
- The home was dark at the time
- Subsequently several lights were turned on, but not in the back bedroom.
- There were three robbers, two white and one black
- Zepeda did see the hand of a black man directing him to keep his face down
- Zepeda heard the voice of the other two and identified the voice as "white"
- Anastasio identified Harris during the incident
- It seemed as though the black male was experienced at robbery
- Harris had come to the house before to see Anastasio
- The incident lasted approximately three to four minutes.
- People in the neighborhood had observed the three men exit a car driven by a female two blocks away.

"Street People" in the neighborhood stated that the black guy was known as "Pig" the street name for Christopher Smith

Zepeda is an Hispanic male, approximately 5'5 tall, and 140 pounds. Zepeda is light skinned, with brown eyes and very short reddish/brownish hair, cut close to his head. Zepeda appears to be pale and is not a very healthy looking individual.

The residence at which Zepeda resides, is an extremely modest, small, one story, two bedroom home, located in the Hispanic barrio. The home is constructed of white stucco and is typical of others in the area. There is no front porch leading into the residence, only front door, which opens and therefore the feeling is the same as walking into a home directly off the street. A small living room dominates the front of the home. Religious artifacts are in plain view inside the home. An unusually large shell drive, big enough to accommodate several vehicles, dominates the front of the residence. There is no garage at the home. Zepeda stated that the robbery took place at approximately 5:30 a.m. Zepeda was in the back bedroom at the home asleep at the time. Someone kicked in the bedroom door in the darkness and said, "Police! Police!" Zepeda stated that he was order to get down on the floor and not to look up. The man who kicked in the door kept saying "Don't look up. Don't look at me." Zepeda said that he was very frightened at the time. Zepeda stated that initially the entire home was dark. During the incident several lights were turned on inside the home. The lights in the back bedroom were not turned on. Zepeda stated that the black man kept talking to him during the incident and giving direction to the other two men involved. Zepeda said that the black man seemed to know what he was doing, as if he had experience in "jacking" (robberies). Zepeda said that the black man kept asking the other two men, "Where is my back up? Where is my back up?" At one point, the black man had a gun on Zepeda's neck. One of the white intruders had a gun on his

Zepeda stated that he realized there were only three robbers involved, the black man and the other two, whom he identified as being white. Zepeda said that the other two men were white because he heard their voices and during the incident Anastasio identified on as Keith. Zepeda stated that Anastasio and Keith knew one another. Zepeda said that Keith had periodically came to the residence before to see Anastasio. Keith would "do tattoos" on Anastasio and on other in the neighborhood. Anastasio was selling crack cocaine out of the house: that was his job. Keith also came to the house to buy crack cocaine from Anastasio. Zepeda stated that he could not identify the robbers. Zepeda said that he never directly looked at any of them. Zepeda did see the hand of the black man as he was directing him to lay face down on the floor. The hand was "Kind of big". Zepeda stated Keith had in fact come to the house the day before the robbery occurred. Zepeda said that Keith had come to the house alone. Zepeda said that Keith came by to speak with Anastasio as he has several times before. Said that Keith came by to speak with Anastasio as he has several times before.

Zepeda stated that the whole time the incident was going on, there were never more than three robbers involved. Zepeda said that no one else came into the house during or after the robbery.

Zepeda stated that one of the white men (believed to be Keith), kept hitting Esmeralda, the wife of his brother, Anastasio. Keith kept saying "Don't look at me. Don't look at me." Zepeda stated that the robbers took money and other valuables. The robbers took tire rims, which Zepeda had earlier purchased from his cousin, Franciso. Zepeda said that the robbers also took Anatasio's gold rings and 1,300 in cash, which Zepeda had with him at the time. The cash was denominated in 100 and in 20 bills.

Zepeda saw nothing of the shooting. At the time, he was in a "face down position." Zepeda only heard one shot. Zepeda stated that Esmeralda told him that Anastasio had gotten up ans was struggling with the shooter. Zepeda did not know who the shooter was and was not told who did the shooting by Esmeralda. During the struggle, the shooter pointed the gun at Anastasio and shot him. All three subsequently left the trailer house. Zepeda stated that after the robbers left the house, they called 9-1-1. Zepeda said that it was 15 to 20 minutes before the police came to the residence. Zepeda said that it seemed as though it was longer than that. Zepeda stated that in his neighborhood "word gets around." Zepeda said that people in the neighborhood later told him that they had observed a car that morning drop off two white men and one black man at a volunteer fire station located at Hershey and Hollywood. Zepeda stated that area resident have told told him that the three men were dropped off at the location just prior to the incident occurring. Zepeada said that he does not know the names of the residents, but described them as two older persons, male and female, who live across the street from the fire station. A women was driving the vehicle in which the three men were seen. A black man, they believe, was someone Known as "Pig" who was identified as one of the three men. The name "Pig" is the street name for Christopher Smith. Zepeda said that he does not know Smith. Zepeda said that he only knows who Smith is. Smith had fathered a baby by a friend known to Zepeda as Virginia Vasquez. Zepeda had seen Smith at the residence of Vasquez several times, but had never spoken to Smith. Zepeda

23

never saw Smith drive through the neighborhood and could not identify any vehicle that he may have driven. Zepeda stated that he could not identify Smith as the person who took part in the robbery that morning.

Zepeda stated that a mechanic who works with his mothers overheard by her saying that an acquaintance of his named "Roe" was involved in the incident and was in jail at the time. Zepeda said that the man said this in front of his mother, not knowing who she was. Zepeda said that his mother told the man "I hope he rot in that jail." Zepeda stated that other than his initial statement to the police given the day of the robbery, he has not spoken with either the police nor has he ever spoken with anyone from the District Attorney's Office. Zepeda stated that Jose Murillo is still incarcerated in the Texas Youth Council in Marlin Texas. Murillo is schedule to serve approximately 20 months in the Texas Youth Council.

Zepeda stated that he would like to have his rings and jewelry back if at all possible

End of Interview.....

Zepeda could recall well and clearly the events that occurred during the robbery that morning. Zepeda was not at all evasive, but appeared to be in control and calm at all times. Zepeda has a good command of the English Language. Zepeda could not directly implicate Christopher Smith in the robbery, but only indirectly from hearsay by area resident.

6 JOSIE MURILLO

Josie Murillo has no criminal history in Harris Country, Texas. During the course of the investigation, it was learned from witness Zepeda and Cordero that Jose Murillo was currently incarcerated in the Texas Youth Council in Marlin, Texas. Zepeda said that Murillo is supposed to be serving 20 months. Investigator subsequently called the Texas Youth Council. Investigator spoke with a representative in the superintendent's office named Dottie.

Dottie stated that "student" have the right to confidentially. Dottie said that she was not allowed to discuss who is or is not at the Texas Youth Council. Dottie would not even be able to confirm if in fact Murillo was at that location.

Dottie stated that the Texas Youth Council could only give direct information regarding "students" to those in his immediate family.

- Cordero first became aware that something was wrong when she heard a loud snap in the early morning hours at her home.
- One of the intruders kicked in her bedroom door
- Cordero recognized the intruder as Keith Harris, although is face was covered at the time. Johnson had visited the residence previously.
- Both Cordero and her husband, Anastasio were ordered to get on the floor.
- There were three intruders in the incident, two white and one black chest. His hair was trimmed in a bald, fade cut.
- Cordero never has seen a photograph of Christopher Smith.
- Cordero recognized the black man in the robbery as the same man who has passed through the neighborhood and waved to both her and Anastasio on several occasion.
- Cordero was concerned at the use of excessive force by the black man against Emmery Zepeda
- One of the intruders, Brad Johnson, began running out and back in the house as he took tire rims, jewelry and money from the residence.
- The black man kept hollering "Where is my back up" during the incident. He was dresses in a black jacket as if he was police officers.
- The three men ripped up the house looking for money and drugs.

- Smith seemed to be the leader in the group
- Both Anastasio and Jose Murillo recognized one of the intruders as "Harris"
- Anastasio became infuriated after Harris hit Cordero with his gun
- Anastasio leaped up and got into an argument with Brad Johnson, During the confrontation he was sot as he and Johnson struggled with a gun.
- A week earlier Harris had stolen $200 from Anastasio at the residence. He later brought a leather jacket and pair of Nike shoes to Anastasio to male amends
- Cordero only saw the same three men inside the home. There was never a fourth.
- When the intruders left the residence, they disappeared almost immediately. Cordero believed the three had left in an SUV.
- rumors had been circulated in the neighborhood that a woman named Samantha drove the getaway vehicle.
- Rumors had been circulated in the neighborhood that a woman named Samantha drove the getaway vehicle.
- Cordero would recognize Christopher Smith if she saw him in a line-up
- Cordero has heard rumors implicating another black man known as "Eight Ball" who is "a rapper" in a local band.
- Cordero believed the intruders may have been "high" on drugs during the incident.
- Anatasio sold Crack from the trailer

Cordero is a young Hispanic woman, approximately 5'4 tall, slender in appearance, with long brown hair pulled back, being light tan in color, with brown eye and very attractive. Cordero dresses well, is very articulate and appears to be very energetic. The home itself is beige in color, with roofing and very imposing. A spacious living room is adjoined by a dining room and kitchen on the northeast quadrant of the ground floor of the home. The interior of the residence is tastefully done in a traditional Spanish motif and appears to be spotlessly clean.

A two-car garage and a neatly trimmed lawn gives the home a distinctly well-planned appearance. Cordero stated that her mother-in-law, Connie Sandoval will always know how to contact her. Cordero was interviewed on Saturday, September 9,2009 by Jim Gambrell.

Cordero stated that the incident which occurred on January 18,2000 happened around 5:00am. Cordero said that her husband's cousin Jose Murillo, happened to be awaken at the time everyone else, including herself, her deceased husband (Anastasio Sandoval) and Emmery Zepeda were asleep. The house was dark at this time. Cordero stated that the first thing she recalled hearing a loud "snap" then a bang. Cordero stated that she then heard footsteps and someone shouting,. "Police, Police."

Cordero stated that Anastasio jump out of bed and flipped on the lights in the bedroom. Cordero said that Anastasio shut the door and tried to hold it tight. Cordero said at that point someone kicked the door open. Cordero said that even though his face was covered, she recognized that person as Keith Harris . Cordero said that she knew it was Johnson because he is very tall and he has visited the residence on numerous occasions before. Cordero stated that Harris talked to her at the time, saying "Stay on the bed" Cordero said that she also recognized Harris by his voice. Cordero stated that Harris order Anastasio to "get on the floor." Cordero said that both she and Anastasio knew at the time that their attacker was Harris, although he was wearing a cover over his face. Cordero stated that there were three intruders in all. Cordero said that the first was Harris, the second was a very short white male, and the third was a black man. Cordero said that she later identified the short white male, because she picked him out of a photo spread shown to her by police. Cordero said that when she saw how short the man was and saw the picture, she knew that it was someone known to her as Brad Johnson. Cordero stated that the black man was rather large and had a very thick chest. He also had a big head. The man was approximately 5'9 tall to 5'10 tall and approximately 250 to 260 pounds, about the same size as Anastasio. Cordero stated that the man had a "bald, fade hair cut." Cordero said that she does not remember if he had a goatee. Cordero stated that Anastasio had a cousin named Franciso. Cordero said that Francisco's wife was shown a photography by Connie Sandoval, the mother of Anastasio. That photography was given to her by the police.

Francisco's wife, named Jennifer, recognize the man in the photograph as being a suspect in the robbery. Cordero said that it was a man by the name of Brad Johnson. The photocopy shown to Jennifer described Johnson by height and weight. Jennifer told Cordero that she used to go with Johnson. Cordero said that she has been given the photocopy by the Homicide police. Cordero said that she never saw the photography of Johnson. Cordero stated that she recognized that the black male in her residence that night was the same male who would pass through the neighborhood in his vehicle. The man would wave to both her and Anastasio, but not in a friendly manner. Cordero said that she interpreted his wave more or less that he was just passing through the neighborhood and he letting everyone know that he was around. Cordero stated that she did not see the other two robbers until she and Anastasio were led out of the bedroom by Keith and into the living room. Cordero, Anastasio and Murillo were made to lay face down on the floor in the living room. Cordero said that Emmery Zepeda was kept in the back bedroom by both the large black male and the shorter white male.

Cordero stated that both of them seemed to be throwing everything around in the bedroom, including Zepeda himself. Cordero was concerned that Zepeda would be harmed. Cordero said that the robbers kept asking "Where are the guns? Where are the drugs? Where is the money"?

Cordero stated that earlier that evening, Zepeda had bought tire rims from Francisco. Cordero said that "Little Brad" (Brad Johnson) grabbed the tire rims and ran outside with them. He then ran in and out of the residence, trying to haul away as much as he could from inside the trailer. Cordero said that Smith kept hollering, "Where is my back up? Where is my back up?"

Cordero stated that Smith kept saying this as if he was a police officer. Cordero said that she believed that he kept saying this to make sure that everyone would remain quiet. Cordero stated that Smith was dressed in a black jacket, as if he was a police officers. Cordero recalled Murillo looking at her while they were both on the floor and saying, "These men are not the police." Cordero stated that she believed the three men were in the house for approximately 15 to 20 minutes. They went through the house "very well." Cordero said that they ripped everything up, looking for money or drugs. Cordero said that Anastasio sold crack cocaine out of the trailer. Anastasio did not have regular job. Cordero stated that Smith seemed to be the leader in the group. Harris at one point appeared to be getting nervous. Cordero said that Smith told him, "Keep their faces down." Cordero stated that at one point Harris hit her with his gun when he saw her looking at him. Cordero said that Harris did not hurt Her very much. Cordero stated that after Harris hit her, she looked at Anastasio. They were both on the floor at the time. Cordero said that Anastaio and Murillo kept saying, "It is Harris." Cordero said that they did not know the names of the other two robbers at that point. Cordero stated that Anastasio got angry over her being struck by Harris. Anastasio subsequently got up and said "Man quit messing with my woman." Cordero said that the short man, known as Brad Johnson, told Anastasio, "Are you trying to be a bad mother fucker?" Johnson subsequently hit Anastasio with the butt of a shotgun. Cordero said that the two started wrestling over the shotgun and Johnson shot Anastasio. The shooting occurred as both were tugging at the gun. Anastasio was trying to point the barrel of the gun down. "Little Brad" was trying to pull the gun back and subsequently pointed the gun at Anastasio then shot him. Cordero described the incident as something, which seemed to her to be occurring in "slow motion." Cordero stated that approximately one week prior Harris had stolen approximately $200.00 from Anastasio at the residence. Harris had spent the night before at the home. Harris was also known in the community because he would give tattoos to young men in the neighborhood. Many of the tattoos read, "Woodland Acres." Cordero stated that after Harris had stolen the money from Anastasio, he returned and apologized fro having done so. Cordero said that Anatasio told Harris that "everyone makes a mistake and to not to worry about it." Cordero said that four days eariler, Harris returned and brought a leather jacket and a pair of Nike shoes to Anastasio. Cordero said that this merchandise was worth approximately $200. Cordero stated that there were only three men inside the trailer at all times during the robbery for any reason. The only person who entered and left was the short, white male known as Johnson. Cordero stated that after Anastasio was shot, the three robbers jumped out of the house in a hurry and left. Both Zepeda and Murillo went out almost immediately after them but the robbers were already gone. Cordero said that there had to be a vehicle waiting outside for them. Cordero remember Murillo saying that he saw an SUV. Murillo described the SUV to Cordero as being a Chevrolet Tahoe or Ford Explorer. Murillo said that he saw the lights on the vehicle as it sped away from residence. Cordero stated that she has heard rumors through the neighborhood after the robbery that the getaway vehicle was driven by a woman known as Samantha . Cordero stated that she has heard that Samantha has been "bragging" about the robbery. Cordero said that she has seen Samantha in the neighborhood with a boyfriend of hers, whom she does not know. The boyfriend drives a black Honda Civic hatchback. Cordero said that when Samantha has come through the neighborhood, she would look at Cordero. Cordero stated that if she was to see Christopher Smith in a line up or see a photography of him, she believes that she would remember his face. Cordero said that she cannot forget Smith yelling with a loud, booming voice, "Police! Police!" Cordero stated that people in the neighborhood have been saying along that Smith was involved in the incident. it has also going though the neighborhood that Samantha was involved in the incident.

Cordero stated that curiously enough both Smith and Samantha know the same people that she and Anastasio know. Cordero said that she has heard other rumors that implicated a fourth man, black male named "Eight Ball." Cordero said that "Eight Ball." is a rapper in a local band. Cordero reminded that she only saw the same three robbers inside the home the entire time.

Cordero stated that it was her belief that during the robbery the robbers may have been on drugs. This was true of the short, white man who she now knows as Johnson because of his quick, jerky movement and his running in and out the house. Cordero also recalled the excessive force, which Smith used against Zepeda.

Cordero stated that she knows that her next neighbors who had just a week earlier moved into their residence were looking out their window as the incident ended. Cordero said that she saw them looking through their windows. As she came out on the porch, Cordero remembers an Hispanic woman at the window as she came to the door. Cordero said that she does not know their names. When asked later, they denied having seen anything.

Cordero stated that when the police came, they put her, Murillo and Zepeda in a car and took them to the station at Lockwood. Murillo, Zepeda and Cordero gave statements to the police. Afterward, all three were brought back to the residence.

Cordero stated that she has not spoken with the police since giving her statement. When Johnson and Smith were apprehended, Cordero was not asked to make an identification. Cordero said that she has wondered many times why she has not been asked to do so. Cordero said that she does not believe the police have spoken anymore also with Zepeda.

Cordero described the trailer in which she, her deceased husband (Anastasio), and Emmery Zepeda lived in as being approximately ten feet wide and 40 feet long. The trailer was light beige to brown in color and seemed to be in good condition. Cordero said that her bedroom was in the far back end of the trailer. The living room was in the middle section of the trailer, with an adjoining kitchen. The room in which Zepeda slept was up near the small parking lot, adjacent to Hillsboro. The parking lot itself may have been 20 feet deep and 50 feet wide. Cordero said that her trailer was one of two at that location.

Cordero stated that Jose Murillo was coming to town some time in October as a witness to another murder, which occurred in Mach 2000. Murillo former roommate, whom he had been living with since leaving the trailer was also shot and killed at that time. Cordero said that she has been told this information by members of family of the deceased. Cordero said that Murillo may not know at this point that he is being brought to Houston in October.

Although still relatively young, Cordero is mature, well spoken and "thinks fast" in the manner of a streetwise person.

Cordero's narrative during the interview was clear and very descriptive. Cordero remained calm and at all times in control. Cordero answered all questions put to her in a very measured, rapid, staccato fashion,

Cordero is very intense, yet friendly and cooperative.

Cordero makes compelling witness...............

To be continued......

ABOUT THE AUTHOR

Introduction: Cicely Vance is a successful Publicist based out of New York also credited "Cece Vance", perhaps best known for her work with Shiest Bubz,Short Dawg and Gudda Gudda

Biography:

The Publicist known around the world as Cece Vance has stamped her indelible imprint on the music scene born Cicely Vance from Houston, Texas. Cece is primarily known as the woman behind the enormous success of underground labels around the world. Cece was the oldest member of R&B/ Rap group Phavor; their manager was Mrs. Rhonda Jordan (married to Houston Own Scarface).

In 2007 Cece move to New York where she was approached by Marshall Morton to start a Public Relations firm. After starting VanceNyCC Multimedia and doing research on public relations she notices that her staff had everything but a publicist. After taking Media training classes Cece became the head publicist for VanceNyCC Multimedia.

Cece has helped to create career-defining press kits for her artists. Respected beyond the genres of urban and hip hop artists, Cece work as a publicist similarly knows no boundaries. Over the years Cece has worked with various recording artists from major and independent labels, quickly moving around this veteran circle on various prestigious and exclusive levels. While learning

the business of Public Relations, which has proved to be a priceless process, Cece has developed many talents & insights. Moving forward Cece continues to master the art of Public Relations and takes pride in her success at staying ahead of the curve with originality and experimentation.
Cece Motto: All Publicity is good Publicity

www.ingramcontent.com/pod-product-compliance
Lightning Source LLC
Chambersburg PA
CBHW051050030426
42339CB00006B/291